Parables And Pearly Gates

Dale Hatfield

Published by Dale Hatfield, 2021.

PARABLES AND PEARLY GATES

First edition. October 18, 2021.

ISBN: 979-8230438168

Written by Dale Hatfield.

Also by Dale Hatfield

Dancing For God
Sinfully Flawed But Heavenly Bound
Yes God Loves You Too: The Saving Grace Of The Holy Spirit
Parables And Pearly Gates
Sermon On The Mount and Parables
The End Of Eternity

DEDICATION

"You can't wait until life isn't hard anymore to decide to be happy." Jane Warczewski

I recently had a moment of clarity. What became clear to me was how inadequate I am. What also became clear to me is that I don't have to be small and insufficient at all. I can choose to be more than I am and have been.

This moment of clarity happened when I was watching a video of Jane Warczewski, who is possibly better known as Nightbirde, when she auditioned for the America's Got Talent television show. Her story of battling cancer was inspiring and her singing was amazing, but it was something she said almost in passing as an afterthought that caused my heart to beat with more of a purpose than it had just the moment before. She said "you can't wait until life isn't hard any more before you decide to be happy."

I truly hope that everything I do is dedicated to God. But this book is also dedicated to Jane Warczewski

INTRODUCTION

I did not want or intend to write this book. I do have messages I want people to hear and listen to or read. I have written three other books that are eBooks available for free at various online outlets including barnesandnoble.com. They are DANCING FOR GOD and SINFULLY FLAWED BUT HEAVENLY BOUND and YES GOD LOVES YOU TOO, THE SAVING GRACE OF THE HOLY SPIRIT. After I finished each one of those books I believed I had accomplished my mission for that book and revealed some spiritual truths.

I wanted to stop there. Writing a book is not easy. Saying something worth saying is even harder. Getting people to pay attention to what you say or what you have written is hardest of all. I wanted my messages to be about Faith, Hope, and Love. That's a little bit of a cliché I know, but still I believed I could add to the understanding of what they mean and how they should apply in our lives. Maybe I accomplished that, maybe I didn't. Only the reader will know for sure.

When I finished YES GOD LOVES YOU TOO . . . I believed I was done writing. Then I discovered that even though I thought I was finished, my mind was not finished thinking. I continued to have a feeling that traditional Christian teaching is somehow missing the mark. The teaching is getting the basics right; God created everything, Jesus is the Son of God, and once we accept those two things the Holy Spirit helps guide us through life. And yet I believe that even though Christian teaching and doctrine is hitting the target, it is missing the bull's eye. And when it comes to faith and salvation, the bull's eye is something that we can't afford to miss.

Until now I have been hesitant to express those thoughts for fear that I would be ridiculed and shunned, or worse yet, not listened to. But I have been recently reminded that my spiritual obligations are not to a religion or denomination, my obligation is to God. So here I am writing once again.

To give you an idea of what I will talk about in this book here is a partial list of topics I will cover: Creation vs. Big Bang; why did Got stop talking to us directly; does everything in the Bible need to be taken literally; are all of Paul's rules to live by absolute rules from God or are some of them Paul's teachings based on his personal beliefs and the customs of the time; thoughts about Catholicism. That gives you an idea of what you are about to read.

I need to point out that another reason I have hesitated to express myself about these misgivings is the thought that I may be wrong. And if I am wrong I might be doing more harm than good to God. If I am wrong I pray to God that you not read another word. One thing that comforts me is that I am certain God knows I do this out of love for Him and His Son Jesus.

PROLOGUE

Before I begin this discussion I want to talk about what prompted me to present these messages. I sincerely believe I have a responsibility to tell you about my faith and what I believe my mission is. I took on this responsibility when I promised God I would be a messenger.

The short version of the story is that one day after weeks of soul searching and asking God why I was not happy a question popped into my head. I say it popped into my head but I believe it was placed there by God. The question was simple, "what would make you happy?"

It occurred to me that I enjoyed writing so I would like to write. The next thought I had was that I should write. But I was reluctant. What made me think I was good enough to write anything that anyone would want to read? And besides, what would I write about. The next thought I had was that I should write about faith, hope, and love.

I immediately thought this could not be God telling me to write about faith, hope, and love because it was too much of a cliché. Every book ever written about God is about faith, hope, and love. So I ignored the thought. But the though kept occurring to me, so much so that I became frustrated and stopped thinking about what I would write and went for a drive.

I decided to go to the mall. As I walked through the mall I passed a book store that I had been in many times before. I kept walking past the store. But it felt to me like God was telling me to go into the bookstore. I thought it was a crazy thought. Why would God want me to go into a bookstore? But as I kept walking the thought got bigger and bigger. So I relented and went back to the bookstore.

I stood inside the store and thought that if God wanted me here He should show me what He wanted me to see. About two thirds of the way down the aisle I noticed that a light seemed to be shining brighter on one of the shelves. I went to that shelf and it was the shelf where religious books are kept. I thought again this is crazy. I have been here so many times that I subconsciously knew where the religious book shelf would be and my subconscious mind brought me here.

So I started a conversation with God and asked what book He wanted me to see. My eyes immediately went to a Bible. Now I was certain this was crazy. I have several Bibles at home. if God wanted me to see something in the Bible He could have had me think I should read one of my own Bibles. But just in case I asked God that if this was coming from Him the first verse I saw when I opened the Bible would be the message He wanted me to see.

I opened the Bible and the first verse I saw was 1st Corinthians chapter 13 verse 13 "And now abideth faith, hope, charity; these three, but the greatest of these is charity". To Christians charity is the highest form of love. I was dumbfounded. For several weeks I had thought God was telling me to write about faith, hope, and love but resisted the notion. Then I felt like I had been directed by God to this specific passage in the Bible about faith, hope, and love.

I went home and could not get the thought out of my mind. I still resisted. I thought I was not a good enough writer to write something that people would want to read. But then I thought about all the books in libraries and bookstores. I can write as good as some of those authors.

I thought it was arrogant of me to believe that God would want me to write messages for Him. Then the most profound though of my life occurred to me. I thought God said to me "It would not be arrogant of you to think I have called you. It would be arrogant of you to believe I have called you and then not answer that call.

At that moment I promised God I would write messages of faith, hope, and love.

DOES GOD SPEAK TO ME PERSONALLY

I believe the messages I present are inspired by God. For that to happen, God must communicate with me in some way. In this book I will occasionally describe how I spoke with God to get answers to some of my questions.

I want to make it clear that I don't have face to face conversations with God. And I don't hear booming voices in the sky. I haven't ever seen a burning bush, let alone a burning bush that spoke to me.

God communicates with me only after I have communicated with Him. I communicate with God by praying. Sometimes I pray silently, sometimes I pray out loud. And then I wait for the answer. Sometimes the answer happens in the physical world, sometimes silently through my thoughts. Sometimes I get an immediate answer, other times the answer comes over a period of time

An example of the answer coming in the physical world would be if I prayed for God to help me save enough money to vacation in Hawaii next year and sure enough I save enough money to do just that. Many people would say "you wanted to save, you saved enough money to do what you wanted, and God had nothing to do with it". Okay. What you believe is up to you but I believe that without God's help my willpower would have been tested too strongly because of temptation and I would not have saved enough money to go to Hawaii.

Others would say my saving was the result of the placebo effect. In other words I believed God was helping me so my will power was strengthened by this false belief. Once again, okay. If that's what you want to believe that's okay with me. Actually it's not completely okay with me. I wish I could convince you that God helped me because that would mean you believe in God. But I can only tell you what I believe and why and then believing or not believing is up to you.

An example of God communicating with me through my thoughts is me writing this subject that you are reading right now. Before I began writing today, I asked God what I should write about. And as I thought about what to write, it occurred to me that saying I talked to God could possibly sound like I have lost my senses. Some might think that I am like those people who stab another person seventeen times and then say God told them to do it. So my I thought I needed to explain exactly how I talk to God. I believe that thought process even though it occurs only in my mind is directed by the Holy Spirit.

So how do I decide whether I believe something I am thinking is a communication from God or just a thought made up by my own arrogance in believing I know something that I really don't know? First I decide if this thought is related to a question I have asked God to answer. And then I ask if the thought is something Jesus might say. If it is something Jesus might say I believe it is from God, if it is not something I think Jesus might say I believe it is a thought made up by my own mind. For example if I have a thought to stab someone seventeen times, I know that is not something Jesus would ever do or tell me to do so it is not from God.

People who don't believe in God and even some people who do believe in God don't think God communicates with any of us individually. To those who don't believe in God I have no answer that will make you believe God communicates with us. To the other people who believe in God but don't think God communicates with us individually, I have some simple questions. What do you think God does? Do you think God created everything and then retired to a heavenly beach to sip pina coladas and eat bonbons? Do you think He ignores us as if we are a toy that He has grown tired of playing with?

I believe God not only created us but takes special interest in every one of us just like a parent would take special interest in each one of his or her children. And that is why I believe God will answer us when we speak with Him.

GET PERSONAL WITH GOD

If you are like most people your first experience with God was when your parents told you stories of a person who created everything. They may tell you Bible stories like Joseph's coat of many colors and how God parted the Red Sea so the Israelites could escape the Egyptians. Most of the stories they told you were probable about Jesus. They told you Jesus was the son of God. Then they told you that Jesus was also God. But He was not different from God. Jesus was God who became a man. Jesus proved He was God by performing miracles. They also told you Jesus died to save your soul even though you might not have even known what a soul is when they told you that part of the story.

Your parents might have also told you about how God might reward you for good behavior or punish you for bad behavior. If your parents went to church you probably learned more about God from a Sunday School Teacher or the Pastor who presided over the service.

As you became older you may have been told you need to develop a personal relationship with Jesus. That changed everything. It was hard enough to understand how Jesus could have been a human at the same time He is God. And now you have to develop a personal relationship with God. Isn't God some huge powerful far off being who might someday destroy you? How are you supposed to develop this personal relationship?

And no one ever seemed to be able to tell you how you should go about developing this personal relationship. They would tell you to pray every day and talk to God about things you need and want. But to you it seemed like the same as writing a letter to someone far away.

I struggled with this "personal relationship" concept for most of my life. Then it occurred to me that I should start by talking to Jesus like I would talk to anyone else in my life. I should talk to Jesus like He is sitting next to me on the couch. I talked about important things like politics and religion and how to get into Heaven. But I also talked to

Jesus about the weather, the football game, or a hard day at work. When I needed help figuring out a problem I told Jesus about it.

At first it didn't seem to be much different from praying to someone far, far away. But then I noticed that out of nowhere I figured out the solution to a problem I was having. And then another thing would happen that I had been thinking about for a while. Then I realized I had talked to Jesus about these things.

It may sound funny or crazy but it seemed to me like Jesus was right there answering my questions and giving advice. And then I realized that it felt to me like Jesus was there whenever I wanted someone to be there.

I began to thank Jesus when I saw a car out of the corner of my eye that was going too fast to stop at a red light and I hit my brakes to keep from hitting that car. I thanked Jesus when I realized I didn't have my keys in my pocket just before I locked the door.

And one day I realized I had developed a personal relationship with Jesus. It seemed too easy to me. But I felt certain that Jesus and I communicated every day, anytime I wanted someone to talk to.

I also realized what a privilege it is to have Jesus nearby all the time. But I also realized that even though Jesus was my friend, He will also be my judge someday. So as I talk to Jesus like I talk to any friend I may have I continue to understand that Jesus is God, the creator of everything and one day He will be the judge of my eternal destiny.

AFTER THIS

What is more important this or what comes after this? The "this" I am referring to is life. Is the time we are alive as human beings on this Earth the total extent of our existence or is there an existence after our human lives end? That is the next question I asked after I decided there is a God.

I decided there is an after this. After I die I will no longer exist as a human being but I will exist as something. But what will I be? The easiest answer to that is I will exist as a spirit. But what exactly is a spirit. Is a spirit alive? Is it a ghost? Do all spirits become angels? I think it is impossible to know for sure until we are there . . . after this.

After I thought about spirits I began to think about eternity. Is it possible to understand how long eternity is? Or is our understanding of eternity limited to thinking that eternity never ends. The only thing I know for certain about eternity is that my existence as a spirit will be longer than my existence as a human being.

I tried to visualize those two things; my existence as a human and my existence as a spirit. The only way I could do that is to picture a yardstick that extends to infinity before I was born and extends to infinity after I die. And I wondered if I could ever see this yardstick how would I identify where my human existence appeared on the yardstick.

On a normal yardstick there are marks; a sixteenth of an inch, an eighth of an inch, a quarter of an inch, half an inch, an inch, and so on. If I want to pinpoint where three inches is on the yardstick I could easily do that. If I were to look at an eternal yardstick would I be able to pinpoint where my human life appears on that eternal yardstick. I don't think I could because the time of my human life would be a teeny tiny speck on the yardstick of eternity. But it would be easy to see my spiritual existence on the yardstick because it would extend from the time I was born until forever.

But God can easily pinpoint both of my existences on the eternal yardstick. God can pinpoint the exact mark where my human life began.

And God can see where my human existence begins and ends and where my spiritual existence begins and can see that it extends forever.

Think about that. Of the two existences each of us will have which one is more important to God, human or spirit? Our spiritual existence is more important to God because that is our true existence. That does not mean our human existence is not important to God. God wants every human being to have everything we need to be happy and secure.

If you doubt that then tell me what God did not provide for us when He created us. God gave us every resource we would ever need. If we look around today we can see that our clean air supply is becoming limited, our clean water supply is becoming limited. Our wealth is controlled by only a few of us to the exclusion of many of us. But God did not limit clean air and water. God did not distribute the wealth to only a few of us. We have done those things. God gave us everything we need to live happy and healthy lives. That is the proof of God's love for our human existence.

But let's get back to the yardstick. God gave humans the gift of free will and because of that the gift of self determination. Only you control what happens after this. God knew that free will meant some people would abuse the life and resources He gave us. And because of that some of us would suffer pain and heartache. And some of us would be mean, even evil. But because God loves each of us He gives us until our last human breath to save ourselves by loving Him and accepting Jesus as our savior.

Some of us will suffer in this human existence. And because God loves us it hurts Him to see us hurt. But from God's perspective looking down on the yardstick of our existence, human and spiritual, the human part of that existence lasts less than the snap of God's fingers.

We can get an idea of how long the snap of a finger is. Snap your fingers and you know how long it is. God does not want us to suffer in this life. But God knows that compared to our entire existence our lives as humans are shorter than the snap of His fingers.

Please keep this in mind, God suffers your pain with you. But God does not just suffer your pain. He suffers your friend's pain, and your neighbor's pain, and your family's pain, and the pain of every person who has ever lived. But God endures that pain in the hope that you will save yourself in the end. And after this human life you will be happy throughout all eternity.

MISSING THE TARGET

Have you ever played darts? I have not played darts often but when I did I'm not sure I ever hit the bull's-eye. And I noticed that even the best dart players I saw did not hit the bull's-eye very much. The reason I am thinking about a dart and its bull's-eye is I think it is a good analogy of how I believe faith teachers and messengers are usually pretty good at hitting the target but quite often are missing the bull's-eye.

They all get the basic most important message correct. To be saved you have to believe in God and accept Jesus as His son and your personal savior. That's a bull's-eye! But when talking about the Bible and the lessons the Bible teaches they often come close but miss the bull's-eye.

They often focus on the story more than the lesson the story teaches. They are so adamant the story is literally true they move the focus away from the lesson. And when asked about the Bible's obvious contradictions they usually try to rationalize why two different people saw the same thing in a different way. But they have already insisted the Bible was inspired by God. That means the individual books may have been written by different authors but the teller of the story was always God. Why would God give two different versions of the same event?

I believe these teachers and theologians are so dependent on people believing that God is all powerful that they need the stories to be literal acts of God to prove God's omnipotence. But if someone needs proof of God before they will believe in God, they will never have faith because faith is belief in something in which there is no proof.

Getting someone to believe in something you can not prove is hard. If the Bible can not be questioned faith teachers believe they always have evidence that can not be disproved. I believe that insisting people believe un-provable events actually happened chases as many people away from God as it gathers to God.

I believe a community of believers is important to build and strengthen faith in God. And I believe church provides one of the best communities of believers. I also believe the leaders in these churches are delivering an essential and important message. But I also believe that while they are hitting the target, they may be missing the bull's-eye.

At times in this book I present alternative perspectives to traditional doctrine. I want to emphasize that when I depart from traditional doctrine I am focusing on a different perspective than the one presented in traditional doctrine. I do not want to challenge Christian religions as an important foundation to support belief in God and Jesus. I hope these alternate perspectives cause people to see the Bible's lessons are inspired by God.

THE BIBLE: FICTION OR NON-FICTION: TEXTBOOK OR BLUEPRINT

I will present my conclusion about the Bible then I will discuss how I came to this conclusion.

The Bible is a gift from God to be used as a tool and a textbook to teach us how God wants us to behave and live our lives. It is a tool to be used as a tool, not an idol to be worshipped.

I believe that next to prayer, the Bible is the most important tool and resource Christians have to guide them through how to live a truly Christian life. And yet I believe the Bible may be misunderstood and misrepresented, not just by lay people but by ministers and teachers and evangelists.

Is the Bible meant to be a rule book or guide book?. Is it meant to recount history or tell stories that illustrate lessons? Does it point me in a particular direction or does it let me find my own way? What is the purpose of the Bible? Is it supposed to give me spiritual answers or help me figure out what questions to ask?

Yes. The answer is yes to all of those questions. One of the earliest explanations of the Bible that I can recall is that the Bible is something different to every person. At the time I remember thinking "this guy doesn't know what the Bible's purpose is so he gives me a nonsensical answer that sounds intellectual hoping that will satisfy me". Well it did not satisfy me.

But I continued to read the Bible because, as I said earlier, the Bible is one of the two most important tools and resources Christians have to live an obediently Christian life. I decided to at least partially remove the influence of teachers and theologians from the process. I read one Old Testament chapter and one New Testament chapter of the Bible every day. Additionally I sometimes look up a particular verse if I have a specific question. Mostly I do this reading at home, on my own in private. I do occasionally seek the insight of a minister if I have a question about how doctrine interprets a particular point.

When there is something I do not understand or have a question about I turn to the other most important tool and resource, prayer. I ask God questions like was it really necessary to say that after a woman was raped and killed the woman's master tore the woman apart and the various parts were sent to different locations in the land as proof of what bad people had done to her. Couldn't the Bible just say that her master told everyone what had been done and the people went with him to avenge her death? But I don't just ask why something was included or why the description of something had to be so graphic. In this specific case I concluded the woman was already dead and could no longer be hurt and sending parts of her body to various places, the master was emphasizing his plea that she needed to be avenged.

I also ask questions like did the Red Sea really part? Was Jonah really swallowed by a whale and then survived inside the whale for three days? Then I tell God that He must know these stories are going to be hard for many people to believe. Some people will not believe they actually happened. And some people will be turned away by the graphic descriptions of violence and gore.

It has always puzzled me when I hear teachers, ministers, and theologians insist that everything in the Bible is literally true and everything in the Bible must be believed as happening exactly and only the way the Bible describes. They say yes the Red Sea was parted and yes Jonah was swallowed by a whale, period, no discussion.

An example of a contradiction in the Bible is how different parts of the Bible treat adultery. When God handed down the Ten Commandments to Moses in the book of Exodus "Thou shalt not commit adultery" was one of those commandments. But in Deuteronomy when Moses was handing down the rules to live by he told the Israelites that if a man had two wives the first born male was to be the heir even if that first born was not by his favorite wife. The allowance to have more than one wife seems to contradict the prohibition against adultery.

I don't believe it is possible to obey the commandment against adultery and have two wives. So what do I do if I am to take everything the Bible says literally?

Christians believe Jesus is God incarnate, born of a human mother and, at least during His time on Earth, a human Himself. Jesus taught many of His lessons using parables. A parable is a simple story used to illustrate a moral or spiritual lesson. If Jesus is indeed God, which I believe He is, and Jesus taught by using parables does it not make sense that God may have used parables to teach His lessons?

There are times when one passage in the Bible contradicts another passage in the Bible. A specific example of this is the book of Matthew talks about the two thieves who were crucified with Jesus and describes BOTH thieves as mocking Jesus. When the book of Luke talks about the two thieves it describes the second thief as rebuking the first for his mocking and then asking Jesus to forgive him. The two versions seem to contradict one another. When asked about this apparent contradiction the usual answer is that two different people see the same thing differently. It both authors were inspired to tell the story by God wouldn't God inspire the same version of the story to both authors?

The Bible forbids eating shellfish but when you ask an expert or authority why they don't condemn eating shellfish, they stumble to find an answer. Or if they do answer they often say well that was from the old Testament and was superseded by the New Testament. Okay, then why do you believe it is okay for women to braid their hair or wear gold and pearls even though 1st Timothy, a New Testament book says they should not do that.

Paul says that women should not have leadership roles in the church but the Bible itself mentions several women leaders. One such example is Deborah who was a prophetess and a judge. A judge in the Bible was a ruler, probably a military leader, and someone who presided over legal proceedings. Another example of a woman leader in the Bible is when King Josiah was told what was in the book of the law he realized that the law was not being followed. So King Josiah sent a delegation to consult with Huldah, a prophetess who told them what God was going to do about the disobedience.

Clearly God allowed women to have leadership roles but Paul preferred they not be allowed to be leaders.

I have come to believe that it does not matter if Jonah was actually swallowed by the whale or not. What matters is what the story of Jonah is trying to teach. That lesson is that if God wants you to do something, God will make sure you do it. And it does not matter if God actually parted the Red Sea to save the Israelites from the pursuing Egyptians. What matters is the lesson the story of the parting of the Red Sea is trying to teach. That lesson is that if God wants to protect you from something He will protect you.

The great commission that Jesus gave to His followers was to tell His story and teach the gospel. Insisting that people worship God in a certain and specific way turns away as many people as it gathers.

We need to teach who God is. We need to teach that God loves us and wants to save us. We need to teach that Jesus taught us how to live and how to think and how to act.

Having said all of this, I have a disclaimer. I believe it is entirely possible that God parted the Red Sea as described in the Bible. And I also believe it is entirely possible that Jonah was swallowed by a whale and survived. I believe these things because I believe there is nothing God cannot do. If God wanted those things to happen, they happened.

But I also wholeheartedly believe it is a mistake to say someone who has trouble believing those things actually happened is somehow less of a Christian than those who do believe them.

If I get to Heaven and discover they are only stories and did not really happen, will I refuse to be saved. No! When I read the Bible I look for

God's intent and ask what God is trying to say in this particular passage? And if I am confused about what the answer may be, I pray to God for enlightenment.

OLD TESTAMENT GOD VS NEW TESTAMENT GOD

One of the things that has always puzzled me is the seeming difference between God in the Old Testament and God in the New Testament. In the Old Testament God expected people to be put to death for adultery, disrespecting one's father or mother. A person thought to be a false prophet was to be put to death. A woman who touched a man's genitals who was not her husband was to have her hand cut off, even if she did so trying to defend her husband against an attacker.

There are several instances described in the Old Testament where God told the Israelites to totally annihilate and entire group of people. In the book of Deuteronomy God tells the Israelites to utterly destroy the Hittites, Amorites, Canaanites, Perizzites, Hivities, and Jebusites. God tells the Israelites to leave nothing alive that breathes.

God brought on the great flood to destroy all of mankind except Noah and his family. God destroyed Sodom and Gomorrah.

Yet in the New Testament God was inclined to show mercy rather than destruction. Jesus, who was God incarnate, said we should forgive transgressions against us seven times seventy times. Seven times seventy is meant to mean to signify that you should always forgive transgressions not matter how many there may be. When given a chance to obey the law that required an adulteress be stoned to death Jesus chose to ask anyone who had never committed a sin to cast the first stone. Jesus knew that meant no one except Himself should cast a stone at the adulteress. Jesus did not cast a stone. Instead He chose to show mercy to the woman.

I don't know the answer to why there seems to be a change in personality between the God of the Old Testament and the God of the New Testament. And it's okay not to know the answer. The closest answer I can think of is that once God became a person He could feel the things that humans feel; things like heat and cold, hunger, sleepiness, physical and emotional pain. Maybe God decided that it was hard for humans not to screw up. In fact maybe He found out it was impossible.

I suspect God already knew that which is why He sent Jesus to save us. But maybe once God experienced those things first hand God became a more compassionate God.

I don't know why Old Testament God seemed to be mean and New Testament God seemed to be nice. I really don't know. What I do know is the God that I have always known is a loving, caring, compassionate, merciful God.

And I'm pretty sure that the loving, caring, compassionate, merciful God is the one I will meet on my judgment day.

CREATION VERSUS BIG BANG

There is debate about whether every material thing we can see and touch was the result of creation by an all powerful God or the result of a cosmic Big Bang. Creation versus the Big Bang is one of the oldest "immovable object meets irresistible force arguments" there ever was.

People who believe in creation believe an omnipotent God created our universe and everything in it based on His intelligent design. People who believe that a "big bang" created everything essentially believe our universe began when a single point in space where time and space can not be recognized as separate things began to expand. At first the expansion happened at an un-measurable fast speed and then slowed down. Because the beginning rate of expansion was un-measurable it is referred to as the "big bang". According to the big bang theory the matter within that single point in space was extremely hot and dense. As the matter expanded, it cooled enough so that the building blocks of the universe could begin to develop.

The vast majority of people on each side of this debate are certain their ideas of how things began are correct and neither side wants to compromise in any way. Those who believe God created everything point to the Bible which says God created everything in six days. Those who believe in the big bang think everything took billions of years to become what it is today so the idea of creation in six days is impossible.

One idea that allows for both creation and the possibility of billions of years of development is that the Bible says God's concept of time is different from the human concept of time. So when God explained the beginning of creation He told the story in terms that humans could understand. In other words God described each task as having happened in a segment of time which he described to humans as a day because that is how they could understand the story.

Christians believe Adam was the first human and he was created on the sixth day of creation. In other words on the fifth day there was nothing resembling a human and on the sixth day Adam was created from the dust on the ground and God breathed into his nostrils. Thus there was nothing and then suddenly there was Adam. Those who believe in the Big Bang believe humans evolved from another species, probably fish, into humans based on the theory of evolution. Evolution is the change that happens in a species over several generations. The theory is that man started out as a fish in the water. Then the fish developed the ability to live on land by developing air breathing lungs and limbs for walking and grabbing. Eventually the changes created a human.

I have several unique thoughts about how everything might have come into being. I believe it is possible that both the creation theory and the big bang theory can both be correct even though they seem to contradict one another.

Suppose God used the big bang to start His construction of the universe. Suppose the theory that God chose to name days as His segments of time for creation is correct. The first day or segment of time could have been a flash of light as the superheated dense matter began to expand. The second day or segment of time could have been when the expansion of dense matter created space or sky between objects as those objects separated. The third day or segment of time could have been when the objects became stars and planets or land and sea. The fourth day or segment of time could have been when God singled out one of those objects to be Earth and caused the Sun and the Moon to support the Earth. The fifth day or segment of time could have been when God created sea creatures and flying creatures. On the sixth day or segment of time some sea creatures could have adapted to be able to survive on land and eventually adapted to become human.

Suppose evolution is the method God used to create humans. Christians will say that Adam was sentient and self aware on the day God created him so he could not have evolved from another species. But what if evolution is how humans became humans? There had to be a specific point in time when man became self aware. The specific point in time when man became self aware could be the day Adam became Adam.

So I believe it is it possible God created everything and started it with a big bang?

WHERE'S THE PROOF

One of the questions I hear over and over, and I even used to ask myself, is "where's the proof that God exists"? After all, other than in Bible stories no one has ever seen or touched God or even heard God's voice.

When I used to ask that question I asked God Himself. I did not see God and I could not touch God but I asked the question anyway. You may ask why I would ask God who I was not sure existed if God was actually there. The answer to that question is simple. If God answers God exists.

The answer I sometimes got was that if Ineeded proof to have faith you will never have faith since faith is believing in something you can't see, touch, or here. That may be true but it was also very unsatisfying.

One of the times I was thinking about this question I was also learning that humans breathe in oxygen and one of the things we breathe out is carbon dioxide. At the same time plants take in carbon dioxide and release oxygen into the air. Carbon dioxide helps plants with photosynthesis which creates sugars used as energy by the plant. Photosynthesis also produces oxygen. Oxygen helps humans break down sugar.

Humans use oxygen and produce carbon dioxide when we breathe. Plants use carbon dioxide and produce oxygen through photosynthesis. If you need proof that God exists go out into nature and look around.

If you need more proof than that then ask God to prove Himself. I don't mean rhetorically ask not expecting an answer. Sincerely ask this question, "God if you're there prove you're there". If God does not give you an answer that you can definitively understand, He's not there.

WHO MADE THIS PENCIL

When I asked God to prove to me He exists, he showed me a pencil.

Most scholars and scientists believe that as the material from the big bang expanded the building blocks of life were created. As I understand this theory small molecules began mixing together and eventually assembled the chemical building blocks of life. These building blocks began to replicate. One of the results of this mixing is the creation of DNA. Ninety-nine point nine percent of every human's DNA is the same. This could indicate that we all came from an original source which those scholars and scientists believe are those original molecules that began to mix with one another.

That process seems perfectly okay to me and may very well be how all human life, indeed all life came into being. The problem I have is why many people believe that excludes the possibility of God causing all of this to happen. Those people believe that everything we see is the result of random occurrences that coincidentally created it all.

Here is why that supposition bothers me. If I lay a pencil down on the table and tell those scholars and scientists that the pencil coincidentally happened without any intelligent design they would know that is not possible. They would know that the pencil design had to be part of a thought process. They would also know that the materials needed to produce the pencil would have to be gathered in a methodical thought out way. And then those materials would have to be thoughtfully assembled in such a way as to produce the pencil so it conformed to the original design. In other words they would not believe that a pencil could just happen by coincidence. But they do believe everything we can see and touch can happen by coincidence.

Archeologists and scientists are certain the stone spheres found in Costa Rica are man made. They do not know exactly how they were created or what they were for but they are certain they were man made. One of the reasons for this supposition is that the spheres are almost perfectly round indicating an intelligent design. So if I understand it correctly those spheres have to be intelligently designed but everything else we see and touch happened coincidentally with no intelligent design.

Almost everyone has heard of and seen Stonehenge at lease in pictures. Once again archeologists and scientists are certain that even though they do not know how it was done Stonehenge was created by people using an intelligent design. And again those same archeologists and scientists believe everything else we can see and touch happened coincidentally with no intelligent design.

I believe that the Costa Rica spheres and Stonehenge are part of a man made intelligent design. But I also believe that everything I see and touch, including the Earth's natural resources, every living thing on Earth, the Sun, the Moon, the stars, and anything else that may be out there in space is also part of an intelligent design. The universe is infinitely more complex than stone spheres or Stonehenge . . . or a pencil?

WHY DID GOD STOP SPEAKING TO US

Another question I have always asked is "why did God stop speaking to us". The only people I know who God spoke to were people in the Bible such as Noah, Abraham, Moses, and possibly David. But from what I can tell God abruptly stopped talking to us directly. Why? If God wants us to know He exists it seems to me the best way to do that is to show Himself to us or at least talk to us directly. I have often asked God why He stopped talking to us.

I have read the Bible numerous times. I'm not sure how many times but probably more than half a dozen times. I read one chapter of the Old Testament every day and one chapter of the New Testament every day. And I don't always get the answers to the questions I ask, at least not at the time I ask them. Sometimes I will read the Bible several times and not find the answer to some of the questions I ask. But I find it to be uncanny how often the answer to my question is right there in the pages of the Bible.

I had read the Bible several times since asking the question why God does not speak to us directly anymore and I had not gotten an answer. But the last time I read the story of Moses leading the Israelites out of Egypt and the adventures and ordeals they had during that time I believe I got my answer. The book of Exodus described the people as trembling with fear in the presence of God just before God spoke to the assembly about His commandments. Moses had gathered the people to hear God speak but they asked Moses to tell them what God said but asked him not to let God speak to them personally because they were afraid they would die.

After that, God may have spoken to individual people such as prophets in person and then let the prophets tell the people what God said. But after the people asked God, out of fear, not to speak with them directly I believe God has honored that request.

That does not mean God has abandoned communicating with us. Subsequent events point to how God has chosen to communicate to us since that time. There are two times when God has chosen to speak to us individually. God became a man, Jesus, so he could speak directly to us and teach us how to live without us trembling in fear at His presence. Jesus taught us how to live but more than that Jesus demonstrated by example how life should be lived. After Jesus died, God gives each saved person the Holy Spirit who dwells within our own spirit guiding us in how to live.

So God never stopped talking to us individually. But the key is you have to want to communicate with God, and you have to listen for the answer. Too often the filters we have learned in life act as barriers to our ability to know when God is speaking to us. Barriers like social pressure or our own thoughts and fears keep us from hearing what God is saying. It's not that we don't hear what God is saying. It's that we don't recognize it is God or don't believe it is God speaking to us.

Sometimes we want the answer to be a particular thing so badly that if the answer is not what we want we don't recognize God is communicating with us. Or we may have so many other things going on in our minds that when God does communicate we don't recognize the communication. There are so many things that cause us to believe what we "hear" in our minds is our own random thoughts and not answers from God

The answer to so many seemingly complicated spiritual questions is often quite simple. If you want to speak to God, tell God what you want to say and then wait with quiet, confident patience and God will answer.

DOES THE HOLY TRINITY MEAN THERE ARE THREE GODS

The idea that God exists as a Holy Trinity with three separate identities seems to suggest there are three Gods. Christians believe God is God, Jesus is God, and the Holy Spirit is God. But Christians also believe there is only one true God. That defies logic and seems to make no sense.

Even Christians regard the Holy Trinity as the central mystery of faith. We have trouble understanding how or why God exists in three beings. I have an idea about why God is present as God, as Jesus, and as the Holy Spirit.

In the last chapter I spoke about why God stopped talking to us directly. The simple answer is God's presence as an all powerful being scared us. So God stopped talking to all of us and then talked to only a few of us who were not afraid of the presence of God. Then those prophets would tell us what God said.

That presented a problem. We often did not accept the word of the prophets. We did not believe that God actually talked to them. Sometimes it was because the prophet was a human being and we wondered what was so special about him or her. Other times we did not like what the prophet was telling us that God said so we rejected the message.

To overcome this problem God decided to become a person Himself. He could then directly tell us what He wanted us to know. God was born as Jesus the person and lived a human life so people would not be afraid of His presence. But God also needed to overcome the problem of humans not believing another human could be all powerful. Jesus used miracles like changing water into wine, healing lifelong blindness, and raising people from the dead to prove He was God.

God also had to overcome the problem of sin leading to eternal death. There had to be a consequence of sin and that consequence was damnation to Hell. Since Jesus was God, his life was more valuable to God than all human life throughout all of human history. If Jesus was willing to sacrifice His life as a substitute for our lives Jesus would pay the total of all sinful human debt. Jesus sacrificed His life to pay our sin debt.

Look at it like this. If I owe a mortgage on a house but the mortgage payment is more than I can pay, the bank will take my house. But if someone steps in and says I will pay this person's debt so he can keep his house the entire mortgage is paid and I get to keep my house. Jesus paid the mortgage on our lives.

But when Jesus died the direct line of communication between God and humans was once again disconnected. Something else had to happen for God to be able to communicate with humans in a direct and personal way. To overcome this obstacle God becomes the Holy Spirit and enters the spirit of all those who believe in Him and Jesus and the Holy Spirit. The Holy Spirit tells our spirit what God wants to communicate.

And the Holy Trinity really is not that far fetched an idea. Humans accept the concept of body, mind, and spirit health. That means that our well being is at its best when our mind, our body, and our spirit are all healthy and well adjusted. Humans have a mind, a body, and a spirit. In the Holy Trinity God is the mind, Jesus is the body, and the Holy Spirit is the Spirit.

THIS RULE APPLIES THAT RULE DOES NOT

One of the questions I have always had is why current Christian religions don't insist on following every rule in the original law. Original laws are the Mosaic Laws handed down by Moses and written in the Torah which is the first five books of the Bible; Genesis, Exodus, Leviticus, Numbers, and Deuteronomy. These religions seem to be fixated on a literal interpretation of the Bible but don not follow many of those original laws.

Mosaic Law required the death penalty for offenses such as adultery, blasphemy, false testimony in capital cases, false prophesy, idolatry, and numerous other offenses. The death penalty would not even be considered in such cases today.

For some time I have wondered why that is, especially in light of the insistence that other things in the Bible be interpreted literally. The other day I believe I found my answer.

When Paul and Barnabas were in Antioch teaching the gospel to the people there some men came from Judea and began to insist that to be saved they would have to be circumcised. Circumcision was a requirement for all Israelite men and part of Mosaic Law. Paul and Barnabas objected to this and a debate ensued. Finally Paul and Barnabas were sent to speak with the elders of the early Christian church about this disagreement.

Paul argued that since God saw fit to give them the Holy Spirit that god had already justified them without the requirement of circumcision. The elders agreed with Paul that it would not be right to place this burden on the gentiles in Antioch or any gentile Christian.

The elders sent a letter with messengers to Antioch which said the necessary rules to follow were to abstain from meat offered as a sacrifice to idols, to abstain from blood, and from sexual immorality. In so doing, the elders of the early Christian church relieved gentile Christians of many of the penalties in the Mosaic Law.

Why would they do this? I believe the Israelite people were God's chosen people. That notion creates jealousy among many non Israelite Christians. But it is true none the less. Christian objections to this notion include the obstinacy and regular disobedience of the Israelites over the course of their history. In truth Israelites are no more obstinate or disobedient than any other people. But more than that, they descended from Abraham.

Of all the people in the Bible, Abraham was the one who obeyed God always even to the point of being willing to sacrifice his son Isaac because God told him to. And Isaac, once he was told of God's instruction that he be sacrificed, relented and was willing to be sacrificed. You may think it was evil of God to ask Abraham to do such a thing. But Abraham knew that God created all life. And God could bring Isaac back to life.

God chose the Israelite people because of Abraham's and Isaac's love and obedience. Because God chose the Israelites and His special people, they were set apart from the rest of us. They were held to a different and higher standard than the rest of us.

I believe that is why the elders of the early Christian church decided that Christians did not have to follow Mosaic Law as strictly as they did.

WHY IS GOD SO MEAN

One question I sometimes hear is "why is God so mean". The question is often followed by an explanation of why the person thinks God is mean. They say a loving God would never condemn someone to Hell. If God was a kind God He would not allow sin to exist in the first place. They say God allows theft, torture, murder, and other horrible things to happen. They say a loving God would never allow hurricanes, or earthquakes, or floods.

In the past I have also asked these questions. As time passed, I thought about what I would do if I wanted to know why a friend of mine did a certain thing. I realized I would ask my friend. So instead of just asking a rhetorical question not really expecting an answer I asked God. I literally asked God "why do you let bad things happen to individual people and why do you let bad things happen to lots of people like when an earthquake happens, or when there is a hurricane or flood.

I did not get an answer right away. Then one day I was thinking about bad people doing bad things to other people. I was reading about a person who tortured and killed another person for no reason other than for his own amusement. And I was mad. I asked God how He could let that happen. I was surprised by what began to enter my thoughts.

I sensed a pain that I had never sensed before. It was not my pain but someone else's. And I sensed that the pain was God's pain. It seemed to me like I was witnessing the kind of pain a parent would have if his or her child had died. And I asked why God would let that happen if it hurt Him so much.

Then God spoke to me about free will. When I say spoke I am not talking about a conversation. I'm speaking about how it seemed like my thoughts were coming from myself and from someone else as well. Anyway God told me that when He created mankind He decided to give man control of his own destiny. And the way He gave mankind that control was to give mankind free will.

Even though I knew what free will is I looked it up in the dictionary. The dictionary I used said free will is a voluntary choice or decision, the power of acting without the constraint of necessity or fate; the ability to act at one's own discretion. And I realized free will was how God allowed each person to actually be free and not be a slave. Free will was actually a gift allowing each person to determine his or her own destiny.

Each individual would have the ability to make his or her own choices. Sometimes those choices are not good. In fact sometimes those choices are evil, and mean, and cruel. But if I take free will away I create a slave.

I also realized that God wanted each person to have the ability at any time to choose to save himself or herself. Each person can choose at any moment in his or her life to be good. At any moment each person can decide they believe in God and change the way he or she lives. That chance needs to be available to each person all the time, right up until that person dies. If the person chooses to believe in God and accept Jesus that person will be saved from destruction.

Unfortunately that means a person can decide to do bad things, even horrible things. And if that person never accepts God the person will be condemned. And God will feel the pain of having lost one of His children.

When God gave each person free will, He saved that person from slavery. Would you want me or someone else to decide every move you make, to decide what you wear, what you eat, where you work, what kind of work you will do, whether you can go camping or not, whether you can go to the movies or not, whether or not you can do anything at all? I don't think so.

God aches for every person who suffers pain or loss of any kind. Every person is God's child. But God also knows that if a person has chosen to believe in God and live the way God wants to the best of his or her ability, God will reward that person with happiness the likes of which he or she could never imagine. And that happiness will last throughout eternity.

So God knows the pain people feel. But God also knows that even when that person dies it is not the end of that person's existence. God hopes that every person who ever dies, whether it is peacefully or violently, will then be happy forever.

God wants each person to have a peaceful and content life. Another person's free will may cause you pain, but God can and will take away that pain and replace it with pleasure and happiness through eternity. Claiming that pleasure and happiness is determined by what you do with your free will.

WHY DOES GOD ALLOW NATURAL DISASTERS

I often hear people say that if God actually is a loving God He would not allow natural disasters like hurricanes, floods, earthquakes, and volcanoes. This is a question I have wrestled with myself. I asked the question many, many times. If I believe God can do anything, and I do, I wondered why God would allow that kind of destruction. I previously talked about how God's gift of free will means people will sometimes do bad things to other people. But natural disasters are not caused by any action taken by mankind. Natural disasters seem like random violent things that destroy property, dash people's dreams, and even kill people.

One day I was thinking about this question and I began thinking about my own life experiences. For some reason I started thinking about living in the Phoenix Arizona area. Phoenix is very dry and if a person wants to have a green grassy lawn they have to perform flood irrigation. Flood irrigation is streaming so much water into your yard that the water stands a few inches deep until it seeps into the ground.

When a person wants to irrigate a yard he or she goes to the city water authority to schedule the irrigation. Beside each road there is an irrigation ditch. Each yard along the road has a gate which remains closed. When you have scheduled an irrigation you open the gate which acts as a damn. The city authority releases the amount of water you have paid for and the water flows through the ditch until it comes to your gate which redirects the water into your yard. Often there are several inches of water standing in the yard until it seeps into the ground. This process allows you to have plush green grass in your yard.

Suppose a flood natural disaster is how God keeps a particular part of the Earth alive and habitable.

I have worked in several health care facilities and one of the procedures I am familiar with because of that is wound debridement.

Debridement is the removal of foreign material or dead tissue from a wound so the wound can heal. The process is often quite brutal and painful. For example if you have a burn that eventually produces dead skin, that skin has to be removed and the area has to be cleansed. The dead skin is cut away and the area is scrubbed clean. This can be difficult and painful. But the process allows new healthy tissue to regenerate so the wound heals.

Suppose hurricanes are the Earths natural way of cleansing an area that might be dying even if that dying process is not noticeable to humans.

The Earth's anatomy is made up of the crust, the mantle, the core, and the inner core. The Earth's crust is made up of solid rocks and minerals. But this solid rock layer is not one spherical piece of hollow rock. It is numerous sections of hard rock and minerals. Earthquakes occur when there is movement between two touching sections of the rock.

What might cause this movement? We know that the Sun provides warmth for the Earth. But we also know that the Earth's core is over nine thousand degrees Fahrenheit. The core sometimes heats the rocks in the Earth's mantle and liquefies it. The liquefied rock is lava that flows. As it flows it moves the section of rock that is floating above it. When two sections of this rock collide it causes an earthquake. But if these sections did not exist to allow for expansion and contraction the single solid surface of the earth might explode or sustain some other catastrophic event.

Suppose the Earth's core has to maintain a temperature of over nine thousand degrees so the Earth's surface maintains a survivable temperature. And suppose the sections of rock are in sections to allow for expansion and contraction. Have you ever noticed how sidewalks are a series of concrete squares and not one continuous sheet of concrete? There is a small gap between each slab of concrete to allow for expansion and contraction. This prevents cracks and holes from developing in the sidewalk.

In this scenario the Earth's core has to be hot enough to maintain the proper surface temperature for life to be sustained. But the Earth also has to have a solid surface for life to live on. The core heat occasionally liquefies the rock above it. The liquefied rock moves the section of mantle above it and this creates earthquakes. Sometimes the liquefied rock finds and outlet and becomes a volcano.

Without the heat of the Earth's core the Earth might not be able to maintain a livable temperature. Suppose the construction of the Earth that allows for earthquakes and volcanoes was designed to ensure the Earth could sustain life.

Natural disasters can sometimes result in disastrous loss of life and destruction of properties. But what if each of these natural occurrences actually happen so all life can survive on Earth?

I know that is a unique out of the box way of thinking. And you may think I am manufacturing excuses for God allowing the loss of life and destruction. If that is what you think tell me how you would have constructed the Earth if you had built it?

DOESN'T GOD HAVE BETTER THINGS TO DO

Someone overhears another person asking God to help that person get enough money to buy a new car. The person may already have a car that works. But the car is ten years old and the person wants a new one. The person who overhears the plea to God for money to buy a car asks "doesn't God have better things to do than give you a new car?"

The answer of course is yes, God does have better things to do than helping that person get a new car. But asking the question implies that you believe God can only do one thing at time. And that supposition is wrong. God can do everything at once. You may have difficulty understanding how God can do every thing at once because you have never met anyone who could do more than two or three things at once. You believe doing everything at once is impossible.

Fujitsu along with Japan's national research institute, Riken, has built a computer that can perform more than 415 petaflops per second. A petaflop is a thousand million million points of operation per second. I can not imagine what even one thousand million million of anything would look like. And yet this computer can do 415 thousand million million things per second.

People can build something that can perform that many things per second. Yet some of us have trouble understanding or even believing God can do it too.

So yes God does have better things to do. But God can help that person get his new car and still do everything else that needs to be done as well. It doesn't mean God will help him get a new car, but it means God can do everything.

HOW CAN GOD HEAR MY PRAYER

Another objection I sometimes hear is that God can not possibly hear our prayers. People can't see God, they can't hear God, and so they believe God is too far away to hear any single prayer. They say that if there is a God He is in the so called Heaven. Since God is not nearby He can't hear what an individual person is saying.

The first thing I point out to the people who say these things is that the Holy Spirit dwells within the spirit of all believers. Because of that God can indeed be everywhere at once.

Many people have trouble believing the Holy Spirit is present in a believer's life all the time. So the second thing I point out is that humans have created cell phones. I can live in the United States and if I have a cell phone I can call a person who lives in Japan and talk to that person in real time. How can I talk to someone who is thousands of miles away? There is nothing connecting my phone to that person's phone. Yet I can have a conversation with that person any time I want.

If I can do that why is it so hard to believe that God can hear our prayers whether He is present with us or not?

WHO GETS THE PRAYER PRIZE

There is an important football game at the local high school tonight. One of the teams is having its pre-game meeting in its respective locker room. The team gets last minute instructions from its coach and just before the team goes out on the field someone says a prayer that everyone on the team does his best and no one gets hurt. Oh and also they pray to win the game. In the other team's locker room the same ritual is performed. That team also prays to win the game.

Only one team can win the game. I have heard people use this example of why it makes no sense to pray. Since only one team can win the game God will only answer one team's prayer. And God will ignore the other team. They say it is cruel to have those kids believe God answers prayers.

In another part of town on that same night a person prays that he will get the job he interviewed for that day. In another part of that same town another person prays to get that same job. Only one of them will get the job. Again some people say it is cruel to make people believe God answers prayers.

Still others say that God may answer prayers but He can only answer one of each of those prayers. How does God decide whose prayer gets answered. My answer is simple. God answers every prayer. God may not grant every wish in every prayer but God answers every prayer.

A human parent has two children. Each child wants to go to summer camp but the parent only has enough money to send one of them. Which child does the parent send to the camp? Another parent has two children who want different video games but the parent only has enough money for one video game. Which child gets the video game that he or she wants?

Parents face these kinds of questions all the time. And they use an infinite number of ways to decide who gets what they want. One child may listen to his or her parents and always do what he or she is told.

The other child is not a bad child but does have a rebellious side and sometimes disobeys the parent. One child may be older than the other. One child may be more hurt by not getting what he or she wants than the other. These are just a few ways parents make these kinds of decisions.

One of the previously mentioned football teams may not get another chance to win the important game while the other team will be back again next year for another chance to win. One of the people praying to get the job might fail if he or she gets it while the other person will do very well at the job. One person may need the money more than the other. There may be another job opening soon that suits one of them better then the other.

Again, these are just some of the ways God my decide who wins the football game or who gets the job and whose prayers will be answered affirmatively by getting what he or she has prayed for and the other person does not get what he or she prayed for.

But God does answer every prayer. No is just as much of an answer as yes.

WHY DOES GOD CARE WHAT I WANT

I sometimes hear people ask "why would God care what I want especially if I want something simple or trivial?" God cares because you care.

Here's an example to illustrate why God cares about everything we care about. A parent is making out a shopping list. The parent puts milk, bread, meat, potatoes, vegetables, cleaning supplies and things like that on the list. The parent's child comes to the parent and asks the parent to put colored pencils on the list. The parent asks why and the child says he or she wants to draw some pictures. The parent adds colored pencils to the shopping list. The parent cared because the child cared.

God is our parent. God created us and wants us to be happy. So God cares about the things we care about. God might not always give us what we want because God knows some things might turn out to be bad for us. For example if a child wants a BB gun the parent might not give the child the BB gun. The child might not be old enough to understand how to be safe with the BB gun or the parent might not want the child to have a gun of any kind.

Parent's care what their children want. God cares what we want for the same reasons.

FAITH SAVES AND WORKS REWARD

Revelation says that on the judgment day great ledgers will be opened. These ledgers are a record of our works. One of the ledgers is the book of life. The things that appear on the positive side of these ledgers are an accounting of the good things each of us has done in our lives. The things that appear on the negative side of the ledgers are an accounting of the bad things we have done in our lives.

The positive side of the ledger only needs to have one thing to outweigh the negative side of the ledger. If you believe in God and accept Jesus as your savior nothing on the negative side of the ledger can outweigh that belief and acceptance. No matter how many things that appear on the negative side of the ledger they can never outweigh belief in God and acceptance of Jesus as your savior. Your ledger will always be positive and you will be saved from eternal damnation.

But is that it? Is that the only determination that will be made on your judgment day? No it is not. The weight of the negative things on your ledger will determine the rewards you receive, and thus the quality of your existence throughout eternity.

Imagine that the greatest reward is that you will live in New Jerusalem where the gates are pearly and the streets are gold. Also included in this greatest reward package is lodging in Jesus' mansion and a seat at the table with Jesus.

If there are no negative things in your ledger, your book of life, you get the greatest reward. But if there are negative things in your ledger, you get something less than the greatest reward. Each negative subtracts from that greatest reward.

What are negative things that will appear in the ledger? Some of those negative things include murder, lying cheating, stealing, and such things as those. But negative things that may appear in the ledger can be as simple as purposefully hurting someone's feelings.

Again, I want to make sure you understand that nothing can outweigh belief in God and acceptance of Jesus. If you have those two things you will be saved. But don't be deceived into thinking that because you are saved you automatically get the pearly gates and golden streets of New Jerusalem.

I believe one of the ways our religious leaders are failing us is they rarely talk about the rewarding grace of works. You will be rewarded according to your works. The Bible is very straightforward on this subject.

In the book of Revelation when Jesus speaks of His return He says that when He returns he will reward every person "according as his works shall be".

WHAT IS RIGHT AND WHAT IS WRONG

How do we decide what is right and what is wrong. Is right or wrong even a decision to make or is the thing that makes something right or wrong constant and absolute? Murder is universally accepted as wrong. But where did that universal standard come from?

Did society decide that murder is wrong and that is what makes it wrong? If society were to decide that murder is okay would that mean that murder is actually right? If there is no absolute authority then whether something is right or wrong is determined by society. In that case murder may be wrong today and right tomorrow.

Are some things determined to be right or wrong by individual authority. For example if a parent says that a child has a 10:00 p.m. curfew is the child wrong when he or she does not observe the curfew?

My conclusion is that the authority on whether something is right or wrong is sometimes a universal authority and sometimes an individual authority. Universal authority can either be absolute and permanent or measured and temporary. The rule that murder will always be wrong under all circumstances comes from an absolute and permanent universal authority. The rule that a person can not drive without a license comes from a measured and temporary universal authority. Individual authority is given to the individual. A parent can set standards of right and wrong as they see fit. Individual authority is usually limited. A parent of one child can not set the curfew for another parent's child.

What happens when it is unclear whether the authority governing a specific thing is universal or individual? What do we do then? Two examples of this dilemma are perhaps the two most divisive subjects in human history; abortion and homosexuality. Different segments of society and culture have attempted to identify the authority on these two subjects. Some cultures and societies say abortion and homosexuality are wrong, other cultures and societies say there is nothing wrong with them.

I do not believe humankind will ever resolve either of these two questions. Regarding abortion, no one knows when life begins. We can use empirical or scientific ideas and theories to speculate but we will never know.

In America we have decided to give temporary universal authority on the question of whether abortion is right or wrong to our government. Which decision the government authority will make depends on which side of the debate has the most votes at the moment. For now the government has given the right to choose abortion over birth to each individual woman. Tomorrow the government may take that individual right to choose abortion away from the individual woman.

There is a specific point in time when life begins. And that specific point in time is absolute and unchangeable. If a pregnancy is terminated before that point in time occurs abortion is not wrong. If a pregnancy is terminated after that point in time murder has happened. Since I do not believe humans can determine or decide when life begins I believe there is a chance murder has occurred every time an abortion happens.

I have not been appointed a judge by either God or humans and therefore I will not condone or condemn abortion. I will always advise against it because I believe there is a chance that the abortion will occur after life has begun.

In America we have decided to give individual authority on the question of whether homosexuality is right or wrong to each individual person.

Again, I have not been appointed a judge by either God or humans. My personal belief is that God wrote evolution into human DNA. And I believe that over time a predisposition to being homosexual may have evolved into some people's DNA. I still do not know whether that means it is okay to practice homosexuality.

I am not a judge and do not want to be. But if God were for some reason to ask me to advise Him on who should be saved and who should be condemned, I would advise God to save everyone. I would say "You are God. You can do anything. That means you can instantly make every persons worthy of salvation. So make every person worthy of salvation". However I would not ask God to excuse sin. I believe disobedience and ignorance should have consequences. I would just ask that the consequences not be eternal damnation.

WHO'S IN AND WHO'S OUT

Adam and Eve ate the forbidden fruit even though they had been told not to by God. Are Adam and Eve in Heaven?

Abraham told the Egyptians that Sarah was his sister. She was his wife but also his half sister because they had the same father. He told the Egyptians she was his sister because he was afraid she was so beautiful they would kill him so they could have her. By telling them she was his sister he put her in jeopardy of committing adultery. Is Abraham in Heaven?

By agreeing to say she was Abraham's sister she exposed herself to committing adultery. Is Sarah in Heaven?

David had sex with Uriah's wife Bathsheba and she became pregnant with David's son Solomon. David tried to deceive Uriah into believing Bathsheba was pregnant with Uriah's son but when Uriah did not have sexual relations with Bathsheba that plan failed. Then David had Uriah placed in battle in such a way that he would surely be killed. So David committed adultery and murder. Is David in Heaven?

Paul in the second book of Timothy admits to being a sinner. Is Paul in Heaven?

If the answer to whether or not these people are saved and therefore in Heaven is yes what does that say about the role of sin with regard to salvation?

The book of Romans, Chapter 9 teaches that God told Moses "I will have mercy on who I will have mercy". God is saying that He is the sole decider of who is saved and who is not saved. Even though God has set down specific rules to live by and not living by those rules is committing a sin, God may still save you.

I have sometimes heard someone say to another person "you're going to go to Hell because you have done this or that or that other thing". And often when I hear that I wonder if God maybe somehow commissioned that person a judge of who gets saved and who doesn't get saved. And

I also wonder if when that person is being saved he or she will decline salvation because God saved another person who he or she did not think should be saved.

I know this. If it were possible for anyone to save himself or herself by not sinning Jesus would never have been born because it would be possible for each person to save himself or herself with no help from Jesus.

So God will save who God will save. And that's that.

A WORD ABOUT CATHOLICISM

I am not a practicing Catholic today. But I once was. I was baptized into the Catholic faith at St. Louis Church in Alexandria Virginia on April 18, 1992.

As I said I am not a practicing Catholic. But the reason I am no longer Catholic is not what you may think. There have been numerous stories recently about members of the Catholic hierarchy committing egregious sins. Many of those stories have been proven true. Also, some people think the Catholic faith is too materialistic, too political, or too strict.

None of those reasons are why I am no longer a practicing Catholic. Before I tell you why let me tell you why I decided to be baptized as a Catholic. It began when I realized I needed an anchor in my life. I was a nomad, traveling from place to place and from job to job. But I was never happy. I always felt there was more to life than just living.

Then one day I realized that I needed an anchor. I did not think that meant I needed to be in one place forever but I needed something I could always count on, something that would always be with me no matter where I might be.

There is a saying that says "no matter where you go, there you are". Well duh! Thanks for that Captain Obvious. But what it means is if you change your circumstances thinking that will change your life, you may be wrong if you don't change yourself. No matter where you go, you are always going to be with yourself. And if your behavior is what is causing your discontent you will continue to do the same things unless you change your ways.

I thought about that for a few days and decided the change I needed to make was to add faith to my life. I had always believed in God but never really paid much attention to God. I decided that I wanted God to always be with me. And I figured the way to do that was to join a religion. But which religion should I join?

I am a methodical person so I made a plan. I would visit numerous churches and talk to ministers and pastors and then choose. So I visited a Baptist church, a Presbyterian church, a Methodist church, an Episcopal church, and so on. I had no intention of visiting a Catholic church because I had some ideas about the Catholic faith that I did not like.

So the day came when I was going to make my final decision and I decided that I would become a Baptist. But I hesitated. And I was not sure why. So I took a walk to think about it. And on that walk I saw St. Louis Catholic Church. That was nothing new. I had seen the church many times before. In fact it was almost within sight of where I was living.

For some reason as I was looking at St. Louis Church that day I began to feel some guilt that I had not even visited a Catholic church when I was deciding what faith to join. So "heck" I said to myself, "to be fair I will talk to a priest at St. Louis Catholic church". Even so I did not think I would ever decide to become Catholic. There were too many things on my list of objections to Catholicism.

So the day came when I was to meet the priest. I have forgotten his name but I will never forget the conversation I had that day. It began like all the other meetings I had. We introduced ourselves and I explained why I was there. He asked me if I believed in God, which of course I did. He asked me if I believed in Jesus, which of course I did.

He asked me some other questions like if I had ever been baptized, if I had ever belonged to another congregation or parish, and things like that. Then I told him I had some concerns about how Catholics practiced their faith. He did not seem surprised by that but wanted me to give him specifics. I brought out my "laundry list" of things I thought the Catholic faith did wrong.

I told him I thought Catholics worshipped Mary and that only God should be worshipped. He said Catholics did not worship Mary. I said but you pray to Mary all the time like she can give you what you want or need. He said Catholics do sometimes ask Mother Mary to intercede for them. Then he explained why. He said that God knows everything and everybody. Out of all the women who have ever lived or who ever will live God chose Mary to be His mother. Then he asked me if Mary were to one day go to God on my behalf, do I think He would listen to her? Suddenly I understood that Catholics don't worship Mary, they revere her.

Then I told him I did not think I needed to confess to a priest to be forgiven for my sins. To my surprise, he agreed. He said only God can forgive sin. But he said that before Jesus ascended into Heaven, he laid hands on Peter and said the powers He had on Earth He was now giving to Peter. He continued to say that whatever Peter loosed on Earth, He would loose in Heaven. He also said the powers He had on earth He was giving to Peter. The evidence of that is in the miracles that Peter performed after Jesus ascended to Heaven. His healing a crippled beggar and raising Tabitha from the dead are two examples.

Peter is historically regarded as the first Catholic Pope. Every generation of priests since Peter has had hands laid on to bestow Jesus' gifts. He went on to say that priests are humans; they can't know what is in your heart. As a Catholic, you agree that when you confess to a priest you do so sincerely. If you sincerely confess all the sins that you are aware you have committed, are remorseful and willing to repent, you will be forgiven. And it is actually God who forgives you.

But he went on to say why he thought confession was a gift from God. He asked me if I had ever prayed to be forgiven but wondered if the thing I did that day was the "last straw". Is this the time that God will not forgive me? Jesus told you that if Peter, and through Peter, the succession of priests says you are forgiven, God will forgive you. He emphasized you must be sincere. The priest is saying if you are sincere in your confession God will forgive you. It is a guarantee.

Then I asked about the body and blood of Christ. Catholics believe the bread is transformed into the body of Christ and the wine is transformed into the blood of Christ. I told him I found that hard to believe. In response, he said that when I was born I probably weighed about six to eight pounds. He estimated that I now weighed about one hundred and seventy pounds which means that I have gained about one hundred and sixty two pounds in my life. I gained that weight by eating. I have probably eaten bread, and meat, and potatoes, and vegetables, and candy, and soda, and so on.

He went on to say that my body is made up of hair, and finger nails, and bones, and organs like heart, and lungs, and pancreas, and intestines and so on. I probably have never eaten a pancreas, or bones, or intestines, or hair, or fingernails. So the food I have eaten over the course of my life has transformed into those things. So he asked why it was so hard to believe that wine and bread can do the same.

He also pointed out that I said I believed in God which means I understand that God can do anything and there is nothing God can not do. So if God wanted the bread and wine to become Jesus' body and blood that is exactly what it would become.

These were certainly perspectives I had never heard before. And I have since spoken to numerous Catholic people who say they have never had those things explained like that to them either. This could explain why many people have bad conceptions about the Catholic faith. I might even say those conceptions are actually misconceptions.

What happened next surprised me. He prayed for my soul and then walked me to the door. What is so special or unusual about that you may ask. Every time I visited other churches the minister or pastor I spoke to wanted me to sign up to become a member of that congregation right then and there. But this Catholic priest was walking me to the door without asking me to become Catholic. When I asked him about that he said that he was convinced that I was saved and that he would someday see me in Heaven. I told him I though he would say I have to follow Catholic rules to be saved. "No" he said, "you don't have to follow Catholic rules to be saved, you have to follow Catholic rules to be Catholic."

I was so impressed with his answers to my questions that I decided to be baptized into the Catholic faith. Over time, I realized I was not disciplined enough to follow all Catholic rules. And I hearkened back to that pries saying I don't have to follow Catholic rules to be saved, but I do have to follow Catholic rules to be Catholic.

As I think about that today, I wonder how many people claim to be Catholic but don't think they need to follow Catholic rules. Those people may be fooling themselves, but they are not fooling God.

DOCTRINE DIFFICULTIES

Religious doctrine is defined as the written body of teachings of a religious group that are generally accepted by that group. I believe there are two religious doctrines that do as much to push people away from God as they do to bring people to God.

The first misguided doctrine is that some stories in the Bible are literally true even if they are very, very, very hard to believe. My personal belief is that God can do anything therefore nothing is impossible for God. But at the same time it is hard for me to wrap my head around someone surviving for three days in the belly of a whale. But many Christian leaders and teachers insist that if you want to be a member of their congregation you must believe it.

I understand it is important for those teachers and leaders to teach the omnipotence of God so they teach there are no limits to the power of God. If these miraculous things are true they are evidence of God's unlimited power and they prove that point. But the need for a blind belief in a miraculous thing seems to indicate a lack of faith not a leap of faith. I have said before if you need proof before you have faith you will never have faith.

Jesus used the miracles He performed to prove He was the Son of God. Even Jesus needed tangible, physically provable evidence of His divinity. But Jesus performed these things in person while people were present to witness them. To teach important lessons Jesus told stories known as parables to teach some of those lessons. The parables Jesus told took place someplace else and were not witnessed by thc people He was speaking to at the time. Since they could not be physically proven they are considered to be parables to teach the lesson.

If teachers insist that people can not view some of the stories in the Bible as parables but must accept them as real occurrences they chase as many people away as they gather.

I have attended some churches that have a doctrine that women must be obedient and subservient to men. They base this doctrine largely on Paul's instruction that women should not be leaders in the church and should defer to men in their daily lives. Yet Deborah is described in the Bible as a prophetess who was a judge of Israel. My interpretation of that is that God had no problem appointing women as prophets and judges.

Whether stories in the Bible are literally true or not is not what is important about the story. What is important is the lesson the story teaches. Whether a leader is a man or a woman or not is not important. What is important is where the leader takes you.

Stop chasing people away. If people will not listen, then they can not hear.

THINGS I UNDERSTAND AND THINGS I DO NOT UNDERSTAND

The God I know is a loving, fair, merciful God. Yet in the Bible there are times when God does violent things I would never consider doing. Some that come to mind are the great flood that destroyed every person except Noah and his family and the destruction of Sodom and Gomorrah. There are other times when God tells people to do things that I would never consider doing. God's instruction to utterly destroy the Hittites, Canaanites, Amorites, Perizzites, and Hivites, comes to mind.

I can not imagine the God I know doing that. I know that many people will be utterly destroyed on judgment day but until then I believe people should not be destroyed. Jesus, who I believe is God's son would never destroy anyone. He demonstrated mercy whenever He was faced with sin.

So I don't understand the difference. What caused the change? But I do understand that God has promised I will be saved if I believe in Him and accept Jesus as my savior. That I do understand.

I believe the Bible is inspired by God. I don't understand how there can be contradictions in the Bible if it is inspired by God. One such contradiction is the book of Mark says that both thieves crucified with Jesus reviled Him while the book of Luke says one reviled Him but the second thief rebuked the first and said they deserved what happened to them but Jesus did not. Another contradiction is the book of Numbers says that all of the original Israelites who left Egypt during the exodus would die before reaching the Promised Land. But in the book of Deuteronomy Moses addresses the Israelites just before they go into the Promised Land and says that they were witnesses to the miraculous plagues God brought on Egypt so Pharaoh would let them go. If all the people Israelites who exited Egypt died in the desert, how could those

Israelites have witnessed the plagues that caused the Pharaoh to let the Israelites go?

If every word in the Bible is inspired by God why do these contradictions exist? If the stories were inspired by God, and only God wouldn't the stories be the same? This is a legitimate question. One possible answer is that the story is inspired by God to teach history and teach a lesson. It's that lesson that is inspired, not every single word of the story. When two different people teach the inspired lesson they may have different perspectives but the lesson is still the same.

I don't understand how Jesus can be God but still be separate from God. The evidence of Jesus' physical separation from God is Jesus' response when a certain ruler asked Him what the ruler needed to do to inherit eternal life. Jesus said "why callest thou me good? None is good, save one, that is God". I believe God can do anything. So I believe it is possible for God and Jesus to be separate and yet still the same being. But I don't understand how God makes it happen.

I don't understand why people insist that I have to believe Jonah was swallowed by a whale and survived in the belly of that whale for three days. I don't understand why people insist I must believe God literally parted the Red Sea for the Israelites to escape the Egyptians. Again I don't believe anything is impossible for God so if God wanted those things to happen they happened.

But the truth is if someone told me today they were swallowed by a whale and survived inside that whale for three days I would not believe it. If someone told me they saw the Red Sea part long enough for 600,000 Israelites to cross the sea and then suddenly the parting collapsed to kill the pursuing Egyptians, I would not believe the person actually saw it.

I do believe there is a lesson in both of those stories. Jonah was trying to run away because God wanted him to do something he did not want to do. The story of being swallowed by the whale teaches the lesson that if God wants you to do something, you can not run away from God and not do it. The story of the parting of the Red Sea teaches the lesson that if God wants to protect you God will protect you.

The stories don't have to have literally happened to teach the lesson.

My conclusion about all of these things is that I don't have to understand everything about the story of creation and the existence of God. But I do have to decide whether I believe in creation and God.

I believe God created everything I see and know exists because of the infinite number of things that had to happen for those things to exist. Something as simple as the Sun being exactly as far away as it has to be to sustain life on Earth is one of those things. The fact that humans need oxygen to survive and we get oxygen when we breathe. That oxygen seems to come, at least in part from plants. When we breathe out we expel nitrogen and plants need nitrogen to survive. We need oxygen, plants produce oxygen; plants need nitrogen, we produce nitrogen.

Those are just two examples of the thousands of things, perhaps millions of things that had to happen and must continue happening just right for us to survive. To me that suggest intelligent design, not random chance.

Also by Dale Hatfield

Dancing For God
Sinfully Flawed But Heavenly Bound
Yes God Loves You Too: The Saving Grace Of The Holy Spirit
Parables And Pearly Gates
Sermon On The Mount and Parables
The End Of Eternity

www.ingramcontent.com/pod-product-compliance
Lightning Source LLC
LaVergne TN
LVHW090128160826
845673LV00015B/1107
9798230438168